DAYS OF TRAGEDY

The Assassination of a Candidate:
ROBERT F. KENNEDY

Written by:
Sue L. Hamilton

1

Published by Abdo & Daughters, 6537 Cecilia Circle, Bloomington, Minnesota 55435

Library bound edition distributed by Rockbottom Books, Pentagon Tower, P.O. Box 36036, Minneapolis, Minnesota 55435

Library of Congress Number: 89-084905   ISBN: 0-939179-57-1

Cover Photo by: Bettmann Archive
Inside Photos by: Bettmann Archive

Edited by: John C. Hamilton

FORWARD

June 5, 1968 12:15 a.m.

With a smile on his face and a bounce in his step, Robert Kennedy walked out of the service elevator and through the kitchen of Los Angeles' Hotel Ambassador. He had reason to be happy. He was running for the right to be the Democratic Presidential candidate and tonight he had won two important states: California and South Dakota.

Walking into the hot lights of the Embassy Ballroom, Senator Kennedy was greeted by hundreds of people who had worked to help him win. The happiness, however, was not shared by one 24-year-old man standing in the nearby kitchen. His black eyes looked nervously around, as he clutched what appeared to be a rolled-up poster. Sirhan Sirhan, a short, slim, dark-haired Jordanian man who had lived for the past 11 years in America, waited for Kennedy's speech to end.

"Is Kennedy coming through here?" asked Sirhan to one of the kitchen helpers, Jesus Perez, for the third time.

Perez wasn't sure, but he was busy, and he wished the guy would get out of his way.

"...My thanks to all of you, and on to Chicago," finished Kennedy in the ballroom. His fans pressed closer, everyone wanting to shake his hand. Kennedy began to move forward. He would meet with reporters and photographers next. The shortest way to the press room was through the kitchen.

With his wife, Ethel, behind him, Kennedy moved into the kitchen, smiling and shaking hands as well-wishers shouted, "We want Bobby!" Suddenly, the screams of happiness stopped short as eight shots rang out.

Like a shock wave, the sea of smiling faces filled with panic and horror. Robert F. Kennedy lay on the floor of the kitchen in a pool of his own blood. Three shots had hit him. Five other bullets had struck people standing nearby. Even as blood poured from his head, Kennedy whispered, "Is everybody safe? Okay?"

Several people were hurt, but not seriously. Robert Kennedy was not as lucky. He would live for 25 hours. And, like his brother, President John F. Kennedy, he would die from the tragic violence of an assassin's bullet.

CHAPTER 1 — RFK FOR PRESIDENT

Robert Francis Kennedy was born on November 20, 1925 in Brookline, Massachusetts. He was the seventh of nine children. He had to work hard to be noticed in such a large family, and Robert Kennedy was always a hard worker.

After high school, his first duty was to his country. From 1944-1946, Robert Kennedy served in the U.S. Navy, during World War II. He was a seaman aboard the naval destroyer *Joseph P. Kennedy, Jr.* — a ship named after his oldest brother, who had died in 1944 while flying an Air Force bomber in Europe. His brother was due to be sent home shortly, but the young Joe Kennedy

Top Right: Robert

had volunteered for the dangerous mission anyway. The plane exploded. Joe's body was never found. He was the first of the Kennedy brothers' tragedies.

After the war, Robert went to Harvard University, and then to the University of Virginia Law School. While there, he married Ethel Skakel on June 17, 1950. Together, they would have ten children, and an 11th was born seven months after Kennedy was killed.

After graduating from law school in 1951, Kennedy worked as a lawyer for the Justice Department. He went on to help his older brother, John F. Kennedy, to become senator for Massachusetts in 1952. Several years later, Robert would help his brother win the presidency. For Robert's knowledge and experience, President John F. Kennedy made his brother Attorney General in 1961. This job meant that Robert would head up the Department of Justice, acting as the top law officer in the United States.

During this time, the early 1960s, black people were fighting for their rights as citizens of the U.S.

Many white people thought blacks weren't as good as whites. As part of his job as Attorney General, Robert Kennedy worked hard for the equality and rights of all people. He made sure that black people had all the safety the law could offer, even when it made many white people angry.

Robert Kennedy also found himself going up against one of the most powerful men in the country, Jimmy Hoffa. Hoffa headed up the Teamsters union. A union is a group of people who have joined together to make sure that they are paid well and that the places where they work are safe and clean. The Teamsters union is one of the largest in the nation. However, Hoffa was running it illegally, stealing and taking bribes. Kennedy wouldn't let Hoffa get away with it, and kept after him until Hoffa was put in jail. For his persistence, Kennedy got a nickname: "Ruthless" Robert Kennedy.

The two brothers worked together almost constantly. President Kennedy respected his younger brother's opinion, and often asked Robert for his advice on difficult decisions that had to be made. The two Kennedy brothers were a team. John Kennedy fully expected that after he

LET'S PUT BOB KENNEDY TO WORK FOR NEW YORK

was finished with his term in office, that Robert would then run as President. John and Robert were not only brothers, but close friends, as well. However, it was late in 1963 that tragedy struck the Kennedy family once again.

On November 22, 1963, President John F. Kennedy was killed by an assassin, Lee Harvey Oswald. Robert lost not only his brother, but his best friend. Losing John hurt like nothing else had. Many sad months passed before Robert pulled himself together and went on, just as he knew his brother would want him to.

The following year, Robert Kennedy won the job of senator from New York. He served as senator until March 16, 1968. On this Saturday he told the country that he was running for the Democratic presidential nomination. It would be a hard race, since he was running against the current vice-president, Hubert H. Humphrey, and Senator Eugene McCarthy of Minnesota. Still, Kennedy was used to fighting hard, and felt sure he could win. If he won the primaries, as this is called, and got the Democratic nomination, he knew he could beat the Republican candidate and become president. He never found out for sure if he could have won.

CHAPTER 2 — THE KILLER

The fourth of five sons, Sirhan Bishara Sirhan was born March 19, 1944, in Jerusalem. As a Christian Arab, he grew up to hate the Jewish Israelis. War raged across his homeland. Each side fought for land they believed was theirs. To Sirhan, it rightfully belonged to the Arabs, and to no one else.

At the age of 13, Sirhan and his family fled the war and moved to the United States. His father, an auto mechanic in Jordan, found that mechanics did not have the respect in the United States that they did in his homeland. After only six months, Bishara Salameh Sirhan returned to Jerusalem, leaving his family behind.

Young Sirhan graduated from high school in Pasadena, California, then went on to college for two years. While there, he came up with what he

thought would be the perfect job — a jockey. His small size and light weight made him perfect for that type of work. Sirhan started out exercising horses at a horse ranch. However, in September 1966, a galloping horse threw him. He fell hard, seriously hurting his back.

Sirhan never got back on another horse. His dreams of becoming a jockey were finished before they ever began. The young Arab had to start over. But what could he do? He began to look for work. The only job he could find was as a stock boy at a health food store. It was a job beneath him. He took it, but soon had a fight with the store's owner and quit.

Sirhan faced the world with hate. For 11 years he had lived in the United States, but it had given him nothing. All he had was his pride and his heritage. He was an Arab, and Jordan was his real homeland. It was this angry young man that began to follow the workings of the government.

One man in particular held Sirhan's attentions — Robert Kennedy. Kennedy seemed capable of doing great work. Sirhan supported him until he heard that Kennedy wanted to send American bombers to Israel to help them fight against the Arabs. Sirhan took this as a blow against him and his country. He had trusted Kennedy, and Kennedy had turned against him. In his notebook on May 18, 1968, Sirhan filled the page with the following:

"R.F.K. must die. R.F.K. must be killed. Robert F. Kennedy must be assassinated. R.F.K. must be assassinated. Robert F. Kennedy must be assassinated before 5 June 68..."

Sirhan had decided what he had to do. On June 4, 1968, he headed for the San Gabriel Valley Gun Club to practice on their gun range. Henry Carreon, one of the club's playground directors, was practicing only five feet away from Sirhan. He noticed Sirhan because of the way the young man was firing his gun. It was the gun club's rules to shoot and pause, but Sirhan was firing shot after shot with no pause in between. He had fired 300-400 times when Carreon approached him.

Curious, Carreon asked, "What kind of gun is that?" Sirhan ignored him. Impatiently, Carreon asked again, "Well, what kind of revolver is it?"

To get rid of him, Sirhan responded, "An Iver Johnson." Shortly thereafter, Sirhan left, never to return.

A few hours later, without any identification, Sirhan sneaked into the Ambassador Hotel. In his possession was over $400 in cash, some change, a comb, a car key, two bullets, a May 26 newspaper article quoting Kennedy's support for Israel, an ad announcing Kennedy's appearance at the Ambassador, a rolled-up Kennedy poster, and a loaded Iver Johnson pistol.

The young man made his way to the kitchen of the hotel. All he had to do was wait for the right moment.

CHAPTER 3 — A WIN AND A LOSS

At 7:00 p.m., Robert Kennedy arrived at the Ambassador Hotel. He had spent the day resting and playing with his wife and six of his kids at Malibu Beach. Now, it was back to work.

His 5th floor room was already filled with nearly 100 aids, friends, and reporters. All were waiting for him. People could vote until 8:00 that night, so the results were not final, but it looked pretty clear that Kennedy would be the winner. Still, Kennedy had lost in Oregon, the state he had campaigned in before coming to California. Knowing defeat, he wouldn't claim victory until the final figures were in.

However, voting *was* over in South Dakota — Kennedy won! It was Vice-President Hubert Humphrey's home state, but Kennedy had succeeded. This was a great win, and Kennedy called Bill Dougherty, his campaign manager there, to thank him.

Just before midnight, Kennedy emerged from his hotel room headquarters. The California polls were closed and the votes were in — Kennedy was the winner! Now, he was on his way to the Embassy Room. There, he'd make a speech and then off to a victory party. Kennedy was looking forward to an evening of fun with his wife and friends. But first, he had to thank the people who had worked so hard for him. Little did he know it would be his last speech.

The speech was simple. He was thankful for eveyone's help, but knew that there was still a lot of work ahead before he became the Democratic candidate. However, for tonight, he was ready to forget the work and enjoy himself. After finishing his speech, he walked down from the platform and headed for the door leading to the elevators. He was to give his speech again in another room a couple of floors down. Before he could get far, he was cut off by Bill Barry, his personal security man. "No, it's been changed," said Bill. "We're going this way," he said, pointing towards the kitchen. The people downstairs had seen his speech on TV, and instead Kennedy was to go right to the press room to talk to reporters.

"Okay," replied Kennedy, as he slowly inched his way forward, smiling and shaking hands all the way. Guiding him was one of the top members of the hotel's staff, Karl Uecker. Stopping while Kennedy shook hands with some of the cooks and other workers, Uecker started to move Kennedy through the kitchen. Suddenly, a small man jumped out from behind a huge ice-making machine, a sinister smile etched on his face.

Uecker, slightly ahead, didn't notice him until it was too late. Kennedy was answering a reporter's question when he saw a sudden movement in front of him.

Sirhan blasted out eight shots from his 22-caliber Iver Johnson pistol. His rapid-fire practice earlier in the day was now being tested. Three bullets hit Robert Kennedy. One flew past his forehead. A second stopped harmlessly in his neck. But the third one blasted up behind his ear and into his brain.

Five other people were also struck by the bullets, but Sirhan didn't care. He had hit his target. At 12:15 a.m. on June 5, 1968, Sirhan watched his enemy fall to the cold concrete floor.

CHAPTER 4 — A MADMAN

"Look out, look out, there's a madman...! He's killing everybody!"
"Get his gun! Get his gun!"

Screams erupted from eveywhere:
"Shots! Shots!"
Unconcerned about their own safety, several people grabbed the killer. It was Roosevelt "Rosey" Grier, the giant Los Angeles Rams football player and good friend to Robert Kennedy, who wrestled the gun from Sirhan's hand. The 5'2" 120-pound Sirhan looked tiny against the huge 6'5" 287-pound All-Pro tackler, but it seemed to take forever before Grier could get the gun away.

Suddenly Sirhan was captured. Someone in the crowd yelled "Kill him!" Other's shouted, "No, keep him alive!" One kitchen worker shouted, "You monster! You'll die for this!" As if just awakening to what was happening, suddenly Sirhan looked scared. The stupid smile he had worn for the past hour was replaced with fear.

As angry threats blasted Sirhan, Kennedy lay on the kitchen floor. Still awake, his head rested on the lap of a young kitchen boy, Juan Romero, whose hand he had been shaking just moments before. Ethel Kennedy, who had been further back, pressed forward. Breaking through the frightened crowd, she walked quietly up to her husband, kneeled down and took his hand.

It was an unbelievable horror. It was also history. Reporters and photographers pressed forward. Mrs. Kennedy begged them, "Please go, please go. Give him room to breathe." They stepped back, but the cameras kept rolling.

An ambulance had arrived. Kennedy was still awake as the ambulance drivers moved the senator onto the stretcher. Pain filled his face as he said, "Oh, no, don't lift me." Then, he fainted. Unconscious, he was brought for emergency treatment to Los Angeles' Central Receiving Hospital, only a mile away. Once there, it was decided to send him to the Good Samaritan Hospital. He'd need the very best if he was going to make it.

CHAPTER 5 — RFK'S LAST FIGHT

As Robert Kennedy lay dying, Sirhan was taken to the North Los Angeles Police Headquarters.

John F. Kennedy's assassin, Lee Harvey Oswald, had himself been murdered only two days after killing the president. Police in Los Angeles were determined that Sirhan was going to live and go on trial. Sirhan was immediately placed in a maximum-security cell. He had a guard in the cell with him, and one outside the door.

Sirhan spent the night being questioned. Robert Kennedy spent the night in surgery. For nearly four hours, doctors operated on the senator's brain, removing tiny pieces of bullet and bone. When they finished, all but one unreachable piece were removed. They knew it would take a miracle for Kennedy to make it. The miracle didn't happen. At 1:44 a.m., June 6, 1968, Senator Robert Francis Kennedy died. He had lived 25 hours, but never woke up from surgery. At the age of 42, he became the third Kennedy brother to die. Tragedy had struck the Kennedy family once again.

CHAPTER 6 — WHO AND WHY?

Sirhan was not answering questions. For 12 hours, police searched to find out who the killer was. They traced the gun's ownership. It was bought in 1963 by Albert Hertz, who gave it to his daughter, Mrs. Robert Westlake of Pasadena. She gave it to a young neighbor, George Erhart. The 18-year-old sold it to a "bushy-haired guy named Joe." "Joe" was found to be Sirhan's 20-year-old brother, Munier Sirhan.

Munier, who had seen pictures of Sirhan on TV, went to the police station and confirmed that it was his brother they had arrested and it was his gun they had. But, he did not know how Sirhan had gotten the gun. In a sad twist of fate, Robert Kennedy had fought strongly for gun control. Now it was too late.

His name and identity now known, Sirhan was charged with murder. Everyone wondered why. Even his father, who hadn't seen his son in ten years, told a reporter, "If my son has done this dirty thing, then let them hang him."

Sirhan knew why. Kennedy supported Israel, an Arab's worst enemy. Kennedy was thus Sirhan's enemy. Through Robert Kennedy, a popular man trying to become president, Sirhan had found a way of venting his anger and making American people take notice of him and his homeland. However, what people saw was not an Arab hero, but a murderer. People hated him and everything about him. He represented needless killing. He should be put away forever.

EPILOGUE

In his notebook, Sirhan wrote that "Robert Kennedy must be killed before June 5, 1968." Kennedy had lived one hour and 44 minutes into June 6; in a way, Sirhan failed.

But Robert Kennedy was gone. Thousands cried for the man who might have become the next president of the United States. From Los Angeles, his body was flown to his senatorial home state of New York. People lined up for hours to pay their last respects to the slain candidate. On Saturday, June 8, 1968 Kennedy was taken via train to Washington, D.C.'s Arlington National Cemetery. He was buried 20 feet from his brother, John F. Kennedy. The two brothers who had been so close in life, were now close in death.

Sirhan Sirhan was found guilty and sentenced to life in prison. He will pay for his violent and senseless act for the rest of his days.

Robert Kennedy, husband, father, senator, and presidential candidate, had plans and ideas. No one will ever know where he might have gone. When once asked if he was worried about being killed, he said, "One must give oneself to the crowd, and from then on...rely on luck." Sadly, Robert Kennedy's luck ran out one dreadful June night in 1968.

SOURCES CONSULTED

"A Flame Burned Fiercely." **Newsweek**, June 17,1968.

"Between Remorse and Renewal." **Newsweek**, June 24, 1968.

Collier, Peter and Horowitz, David. **The Kennedys**. New York: Summit Books 1984.

David, Lester and Irene. **Bobby Kennedy: The Making of a Folk Hero**. New York: Dodd, Mead & Company, 1986.

Emmet, Christopher. "The Media and the Assassinations." **National Review**, July 30, 1968.

Gans, Herbert J. "Why did Kennedy Die?" **Trans-Action**, July/August 1968.

Horowitz, Irving Louis. "Kennedy's Death —Myths and Realities." **Trans-Action**, July/August 1968.

Kaiser, Robert Blair. **RFK Must Die!** New York: E.P. Dutton & Company, Inc., 1970.

Kennedy, Robert F. **Robert F. Kennedy: Promises To Keep**. Missouri: Hallmark Cards, Inc., 1969.

Newfield, Jack. **Robert Kennedy: A Memoir**. New York: E.P. Dutton & Co., Inc., 1969.

Noguchi, Thomas T., M.D. with DiMona, Joseph. **Coroner**. New York: Simon and Schuster, 1983.

"RFK: The Man, the Dream, the Tragedy." **U.S. News & World Report**, June 17, 1968.

Roberts, Allen. **Robert Kennedy: Biography of a Compulsive Politician**. Massachusetts: Branden Press Inc., 1984.

Scheer, Robert. "The Night Bobby Died." **Ramparts**, August 10, 1968.

Wainwright, Loudon. "Suddenly, a Mass of Screaming Men and Women." **Life**, January 17, 1969.

Witcover, Jules. **85 Days The Last Campaign of Robert Kennedy**. New York: Quill, William, Morrow, 1969.

Wallechinsky, David, and Wallace, Irving. **The People's Almanac**. New York: Doubleday & Company, Inc., 1975.

Wallechinsky, David, and Wallace, Irving. **The People's Almanac #2**. New York: Doubleday & Company, Inc., 1978.

White, Theodore H. "The Wearing Last Weeks and a Precious Last Day." **Life**, June 14, 1968.